Longing for the KING

Beyond the Broken

Kendell Easley
Halim Suh

LifeWay Press®
Nashville, Tennessee

© 2014 LifeWay Press®

No part of this work may be reproduced or transmitted in any form or by any means, electronic or mechanical, including photocopying and recording, or by any information storage or retrieval system, except as may be expressly permitted in writing by the publisher. Requests for permission should be addressed in writing to LifeWay Press®, One LifeWay Plaza, Nashville, TN 37234-0152.

Item: 005695955
ISBN: 978-1-4300-3677-7
Dewey decimal classification number: 231.72
Subject heading: JESUS CHRIST--KINGSHIP \ KINGDOM OF GOD \ JESUS CHRIST--SECOND COMING

Eric Geiger
Vice President, Church Resources

Ed Stetzer
General Editor

Trevin Wax
Managing Editor

Faith Whatley
Director, Adult Ministry

Philip Nation
Director, Adult Ministry Publishing

Joel Polk
Content Editor

We believe that the Bible has God for its author; salvation for its end; and truth, without any mixture of error, for its matter and that all Scripture is totally true and trustworthy. To review LifeWay's doctrinal guideline, please visit *www.lifeway.com/doctrinalguideline*.

Unless otherwise noted, all Scripture quotations are taken from the Holman Christian Standard Bible®, copyright 1999, 2000, 2002, 2003, 2009 by Holman Bible Publishers. Used by permission.

For ordering or inquiries, visit *www.lifeway.com;* write LifeWay Small Groups; One LifeWay Plaza; Nashville, TN 37234-0152; or call toll free (800) 458-2772.

Printed in the United States of America.

Adult Ministry Publishing
LifeWay Church Resources
One LifeWay Plaza
Nashville, Tennessee 37234-0152

TABLE OF CONTENTS

ABOUT THE GOSPEL PROJECT AND WRITERS . . 4

HOW TO USE THIS STUDY. 5

SESSION 1:. 6
His Supremacy

SESSION 2: 18
The Enemy's Atrocity

SESSION 3: 30
Our Identity

SESSION 4: 42
Altered Humanity

SESSION 5: 54
Stuck in Mediocrity

SESSION 6: 66
A Future Reality

SMALL-GROUP TIPS AND VALUES 78

ABOUT THE GOSPEL PROJECT

Some people see the Bible as a collection of stories with morals for life application. But it's so much more. Sure, the Bible has some stories in it, but it's also full of poetry, history, codes of law and civilization, songs, prophecy, letters—even a love letter. When you tie it all together, something remarkable happens. A story is revealed. One story. The story of redemption through Jesus. This is *The Gospel Project*.

When we begin to see the Bible as the story of redemption through Jesus Christ, God's plan to rescue the world from sin and death, our perspective changes. We no longer look primarily for what the Bible says about us but instead see what it tells us about God and what He has done. After all, it's the gospel that saves us, and when we encounter Jesus in the pages of Scripture, the gospel works on us, transforming us into His image. *We become God's gospel project.*

ABOUT THE WRITERS

Halim Suh and his wife, Angela, have three kids and live in Austin, Texas, where he is pastor of teaching and theology at The Austin Stone Community Church. He is the author (with Matt Carter) of two Threads studies: *Creation Unraveled* and *Creation Restored*. Halim has a Master of Divinity from Southwestern Baptist Theological Seminary.

Kendell Easley is a professor of biblical studies at Union University, in Memphis, Tennessee, and is the director of the Master of Christian Studies and Doctor of Ministry programs for Union's Stephen Olford Center. He has written ongoing curriculum for more than 20 years. Kendell is married to Nancy, and they have one married young adult son.

Barry Cram adapted this material for use with small groups.

HOW TO USE THIS STUDY

Welcome to *The Gospel Project*, a gospel-centered small-group study that dives deep into the things of God, lifts up Jesus, focuses on the grand story of Scripture, and drives participants to be on mission. This small-group Bible study provides opportunities to study the Bible and to encounter the living Christ. *The Gospel Project* provides you with tools and resources to purposefully study God's Word and to grow in the faith and knowledge of God's Son. And what's more, you can do so in the company of others, encouraging and building up one another. Here are some things to remember that will help you maximize the usefulness of this resource:

GATHER A GROUP. We grow in the faith best in community with other believers, as we love, encourage, correct, and challenge one another. The life of a disciple of Christ was never meant to be lived alone, in isolation.

PRAY. Pray regularly for your group members.

PREPARE. This resource includes the Bible study content, three devotionals, and discussion questions for each session. Work through the session and devotionals in preparation for each group session. Take notes and record your own questions. Also consider the follow-up questions so you are ready to participate in and add to the discussion, bringing up your own notes and questions where appropriate.

RESOURCE YOURSELF. Make good use of the additional resources available on the Web at *www.gospelproject.com/additionalresources* and search for this specific title. Download a podcast. Read a blog post. Be intentional about learning from others in the faith. For tips on how to better lead groups or additional ideas for leading this Bible study, visit: *www.ministrygrid.com/web/thegospelproject*.

GROUP TIME. Gather together with your group to discuss the session and devotional content. Work through the follow-up questions and your own questions. Discuss the material and the implications for the lives of believers and the mission to which we have been called.

OVERFLOW. Remember … *The Gospel Project* is not just a Bible study. *We* are the project. The gospel is working on us. Don't let your preparation time be simply about the content. Let the truths of God's Word soak in as you study. Let God work on your heart first, and then pray that He will change the hearts of the other people in your group.

THE GOSPEL PROJECT

Session 1

His Supremacy

> Just as millions of angels participated in the dazzling show when the morning stars sang together at creation, so will the innumerable hosts of heaven help bring to pass God's prophetic declarations throughout time and into eternity.[1]
>
> **BILLY GRAHAM**

INDIVIDUAL STUDY

"And the Oscar goes to … " The audience, filled with Hollywood's royalty decked out in its finest attire, holds its collective breath. The speaker pauses dramatically. The winner pretends to be surprised, struts to the podium, and thanks everyone involved in this remarkable outcome. This scene plays out many times at the Academy Awards. And the next year, the cycle repeats itself. Last year's praiseworthy actor begins to fade as the new kings and queens of Hollywood are crowned.

Something in all of us longs to give praise where praise is due. We love to receive praise as well. The trouble is this—praise for human success is so fleeting. Even the most celebrated films eventually make it to the $2.99 bargain bin at the supermarket. It's the same with sports. Who won the FIFA World Cup in 1982 or the World Series in 1992 or the Stanley Cup in 2002? Rarely do you find someone who remembers the winner of major sporting events in the past, much less the winning teams twenty or thirty years ago.

> **When was the last time you praised someone who really deserved it? What had they accomplished?**

> **What emotions did you feel as you praised that person? What was their reaction? Does this emotion fade over time? Why or why not?**

What should we learn from this desire to praise human success? What does this tendency tell us about our worship? Perhaps it's a clue to remind us that Someone does deserve praise—not for temporary success that fades, but for beauty that's everlasting. What if that Someone wants us to know Him? What if He invites us to join with others in offering praise forever?

Over the next few weeks, we'll trace the story of God's kingdom through the Scriptures. This is the story of a Creator worthy of praise, of an Enemy bent on destroying the world, of sinful humans redirecting their praise in all the wrong places, of a King stepping into the chaos to restore His fallen world, and of a people redeemed and set free to live with and for the King forever.

Throughout the week engage these daily study sections on your own. Each centers on a different aspect of God's supremacy. There are three daily readings to prepare you before your group meets for this session. Interact with the Scriptures and be ready to interact with your small group.

Longing for the King

 # God is to be Praised in the Heavens

Before the creation of the universe, many people imagine that God was lonely. But this can't be true. God has always lived in the perfect community of Father, Son, and Holy Spirit. This family, existing beyond limits of time and space, had no loneliness. Everything was perfect.

Then, "in the beginning, God created the heavens and the earth" (Gen. 1:1). Theologians and philosophers have speculated on why He would do such a thing. Thoughtful people have often asked, "Why am I here?" In an attempt to discover an answer, go back to the awards show mentioned earlier. Why do we engage in elaborate efforts to applaud great work? Why do we insist on displaying awesome paintings in museums rather than hiding them in closets? Why do we develop special medals and awards for persons who have excelled at doing good? Quite simply, the answer is that beauty—all that is great and true—deserves widespread recognition. And because God is truly the greatest, He deserves the greatest praise.

> You are matchless, O Lord. So our praise of You must rise above
> our humanity ... You awaken in us a delight at praising You.[2]
> **AUGUSTINE (354-430)**

It was a good thing for God's greatness, goodness, and love to be admired and praised—that's why He created the world! While some may think it was selfish of God to desire praise, we know that such a desire is no more selfish than a wonderful musician to bask in the applause after he concludes a concert. One goal of a performer is that his listeners will experience pleasure. And when the audience is pleased, he is pleased. As we praise God, we are filled with joy, and He is pleased. For we have an audience of One.

> [1] Hallelujah!
> Praise the LORD from the heavens; praise Him in the heights.
> [2] Praise Him, all His angels; praise Him, all His hosts.
> [3] Praise Him, sun and moon; praise Him, all you shining stars.
> [4] Praise Him, highest heavens, and you waters above the heavens.
> [5] Let them praise the name of Yahweh,
> for He commanded, and they were created.
> [6] He set them in position forever and ever;
> He gave an order that will never pass away.
> **PSALM 148:1-6**

The Word of God has always been powerful. When He created, He determined also to sustain His creation. He set the heavens in order in a way to preserve them, putting them in their position forever. What we often have called "the laws of nature" is actually God's Word continuing to have force in every aspect of time and space.

In ancient days, people identified three "heavens." The first heaven is the sky we experience—birds, clouds, wind, and rain. The second heaven very few have personally experienced—space and moon, planets and stars. The third heaven is the very dwelling place of God.

How does the creation of entities in the three heavens show God's power?

In your experience, what elements in each of the three heavens especially display the majesty of their Creator?

This psalm gives attention to all three heavens, beginning with the highest heaven and moving downward. Verse 2 recalls that the "angels" and the "hosts" (heavenly armies) of the Lord were designed to praise their Maker. As they fulfilled their God-ordained responsibilities—communicating messages and engaging in spiritual warfare—they brought Him praise.

The second heaven—the "sun and moon" and "shining stars"—bring praise to the One who created them. Genesis accounts that these were made on the fourth day (Gen. 1:16-19). No less than the angels, the sun, moon, and stars were created to extol the One who made them.

Every line of Psalm 148:1-4 begins with the Hebrew *hallelu* ("praise"). In verse 4 the "waters" in the heavens are called on to praise Him. Clouds and rain and hail and snow call forth God's praises. From a meteorological perspective, we understand that such atmospheric waters are above the heavens in the sense that they're farther up than we can reach out and touch.

What can you draw from the truth that even creation itself worships God?

Longing for the King

2 God is to be Praised on Earth

⁷ Praise the LORD from the earth, all sea monsters and ocean depths,
⁸ lightning and hail, snow and cloud,
powerful wind that executes His command,
⁹ mountains and all hills, fruit trees and all cedars,
¹⁰ wild animals and all cattle, creatures that crawl and flying birds,
¹¹ kings of the earth and all peoples, princes and all judges of the earth,
¹² young men as well as young women, old and young together.
¹³ Let them praise the name of Yahweh, for His name alone is exalted.
His majesty covers heaven and earth.
¹⁴ He has raised up a horn for His people,
resulting in praise to all His godly ones,
to the Israelites, the people close to Him.
Hallelujah!
PSALM 148:7-14

The second half of Psalm 148 opens with a call for the earthly portion of God's creation to praise Him. Notice that the imperative verb *praise* extends throughout the rest of the psalm to include all earthly beings—animate or inanimate. There were sea monsters and creatures in the "ocean depths," hidden from human eyes, whose purpose even in the abyss was to praise their Maker. He made the birds and winged creatures that would share the atmosphere with lightning, hail, snow, cloud, and winds—all of them praising the name of Yahweh.

What the psalmist knew (and we modern people easily forget) is that God designed weather phenomena to accomplish His purposes; therefore, even the weather gives Him glory. As each element does its thing, it "executes His command." Weather isn't random or impersonal after all.

The "mountains and all hills" and all vegetation were created on the third day (Gen. 1:11-13; Ps. 148:9). In verse 10, the psalmist noted groups within the animal kingdom were created to praise God. The psalmist concluded the animals by mentioning "flying birds," which belong to the fifth day of creation. Perhaps they came last because birds singing can so easily be understood as voices lifted in praise to the Maker.

> **What elements of God's majesty do you see displayed in the earthly part of creation?**

His Supremacy

> How does observing these elements help us in witnessing to others about God's greatness and love?

Verses 11-12 describe a kaleidoscope of human diversity—humans made in the image of God—all of whom are called to praise Him. It includes those with power ("kings," "princes," and "judges"). It includes ordinary individuals ("all peoples"). It includes all age groups. It includes male and female. All are exhorted to praise Yahweh. Watch how the psalmist moved beyond the mere fact of creation to the reasons for worship:

- Earth is to praise "the name of Yahweh" because God has the most exalted name and reputation in the universe. Among other things, *name* stands for character and reputation.

- Earth is to praise Him because of "His majesty" in all the earth. The grandeur of earth, and therefore its Creator, can be seen in every crevice in the world. Like a blanket, His creative splendor covers everything.

- Earth is to praise Him because He has "raised up a horn" for His people. The horn, a biblical symbol of strength and power, probably stands for salvation, both from sin and from enemies.

The people especially called to praise God are those who have received His wonderful salvation! His people understand His love and power the best. They are to stand and praise. No wonder the psalmist concluded with a final "Hallelujah!" We, who have received His salvation, have as an integral part of our mission to display the glory of God's love and power.

> What is the connection between our worship and our witness? How can observing the universe's praise encourage us to praise God?

> Creation draws us to look at something beyond ourselves and marvel at it. All of creation has been given to us so that we behold the awesome God who has made it all and made it all good.[3]
> **MATT CHANDLER**

3 God was Praised by Angels

In his series of children's fiction books called *The Chronicles of Narnia*, C. S. Lewis imagined what another world was like. He accounted for its creation by telling what some children, including the boy Digory, saw at the beginning of Narnia. *The Magician's Nephew* describes the heavens bursting into song as Aslan (the lion-like Christ figure) sings them into existence: "The voice [of Aslan] was suddenly joined by other voices; ... If you had seen and heard it as Digory did, you would have felt quite certain ... that it was the First Voice, the deep one, which had made them appear and made them sing."[4]

Lewis was on target. At the beginning of creation, God first lavished creative energy on His heavenly home and its inhabitants. This is what we've called earlier in this study "the third heaven." But why create the angelic beings before He created other intelligent life? At least in part, God was making it possible for an adoring audience to observe the rest of His creative acts and to praise Him for them. We find evidence for this in an astonishing passage in Job:

> [5] Who fixed its dimensions? Certainly you know!
> Who stretched a measuring line across it?
> [6] What supports its foundations?
> Or who laid its cornerstone
> [7] while the morning stars sang together
> and all the sons of God shouted for joy?
> JOB 38:5-7

These verses come near the beginning of God's response to Job, a man who had greatly suffered and who had called out to God for answers. God began with a series of rhetorical questions designed to bring Job to an awareness of God the King. Yahweh is the Sovereign Lord.

God's laying out of the earth didn't occur in a vacuum. The observers were angelic beings—"the morning stars" and "the sons of God." God's heavenly court was watching Him as He created the earth with its kaleidoscope of staggering beauty. What was their response? They formed a colossal choir and "sang together" and "shouted for joy." They praised the One who created them because this fulfilled God's purpose in calling them forth.

Consider the following scriptural truths about angels:

- Angels are personal spirit beings created by God. *Personal* means they have intellect, emotions, and will; they can have a relationship with God. *Spirit beings* means their primary mode of existence isn't bodily (2 Kings 6:16-17).

- Angels have both wisdom and strength. They don't know everything and aren't all-powerful. As God's messengers, they carry out His commands (Ps. 91:11).

- The number of angels is fixed but huge. Angels exist in many different orders, such as the cherubim and winged seraphim (Gen. 3:24; Isa. 6:2; Rev. 5:11).

- The "host of heaven" or "heavenly host" refers to angels who are God's warriors. One of His names is "the LORD of hosts," or "Yahweh Sabaoth" (1 Sam. 17:45; Luke 2:13; Jas. 5:4).

- Angels are presented as male (and when they are visible to humans, they look like human men). They're incapable of sexual intimacy or reproduction as humans are (Matt. 22:30).

- Some angels are assigned by God as "ministering spirits" to serve God's people (Heb. 1:14).

- Like the rest of God's creation, angels exist to bring glory and praise to God. Revelation 5–6 portrays angels as worshiping both God on His throne and the Lamb of God.

What images come to mind when you think of angels? How do these images correspond to the biblical teaching about angels?

How would your life be different (attitudes or actions) if you praised God on earth the way the angels praise God in heaven?

Think about the angels who shouted the angelic version of "hallelujah" as they watched God the King create the universe, the world, and everything in them. They've praised Him eternally since: "Day and night they never stop, saying: Holy, holy, holy, Lord God, the Almighty, who was, who is, and who is coming" (Rev. 4:8).

On a daily basis, in what ways do you see yourself joining in the praise that goes on in the highest heavens?

Longing for the King

GROUP STUDY

Warm Up

Because of the ceremonial aspect of "proper church behavior," it's possible that many of us find it difficult to imagine the sounds, sights, and emotions connected to uninhibited, no-holds-barred praise toward God. But instead of looking to the 11 o'clock hour on Sunday to see this, we should be looking for the NFL hour on television. The roar of a sell-out-crowd stadium—and all the raw emotion from the loyal fans—deserves our full attention. Truly, it's a small picture (and symbol) of what we will experience in the future as we gather around the Person of Jesus Christ. John records his revelation and wrote these passages:

> ^{1} Then I saw another mighty angel coming down from heaven. He was robed in a cloud, with a rainbow above his head; his face was like the sun, and his legs were like fiery pillars, ^{2} he was holding a little scroll, which lay open in his hand. He planted his right foot on the sea and his left foot on the land, ^{3} and he gave a loud shout like the roar of a lion. When he shouted, the voices of the seven thunders spoke.
> **REVELATION 10:1-3**

> After this I heard what sounded like the roar of a great multitude in heaven shouting:
> "Hallelujah! Salvation and glory and power belong to our God."
> **REVELATION 19:1**

> And I heard a sound from heaven like the roar of rushing waters and like a loud peal of thunder.
> **REVELATION 14:2**

Eventually, we all will experience the physical, mental, emotional, and spiritual fulfillment that comes from joining in on that holy roar.

Until then, what are some ways we can praise God as we're out in the world—among neighbors, with coworkers, or surrounded by strangers?

Discussion

Before the world existed, God was always there—Father, Son, and Spirit united in love and glory forever. In love, God created everything in heaven and on earth for His glory. As Creator, He is worthy to receive praise from everything in heaven and on earth. The mission of God's people today is driven by a vision of His power and love, both of which He displayed in the creation of the universe.

During this time you'll have an opportunity to discuss what God revealed to you during the week. Listed below are some of the questions from your daily reading assignments. They will guide your small-group discussion.

1. What emotions did you feel as you praised someone who really deserved it? What was their reaction? Does this emotion fade over time? Why or why not?

2. In what ways has man missed the mark and worshiped God's creation instead of the Creator?

3. How does the creation of entities in the three heavens show God's power? In your experience, what elements in each of the three heavens especially display the majesty of their Creator?

4. What elements of God's majesty do you see displayed in the earthly part of creation?

5. What is the connection between our worship and our witness? How can observing the universe's praise encourage us to praise God?

6. How would your life be different (attitudes or actions) if you praised God on earth the way the angels praise God in heaven?

7. In what ways are you joining in the praise that goes on in the highest heavens?

Conclusion

"And the greatest is ... " No question about it, God the King of heaven and earth is the greatest. He's the most beautiful, the most righteous, the most everything good and pure. He created the heavens in all their complexity, visible and invisible, so that they all would praise Him.

Because Jesus' followers have been made alive to this reality, we're driven by the vision of God's power and love on display in the creation of the universe. What a privilege it is to praise the One who made us for His glory. Our mission is to spread the fame of His name.

Spend some time praying this for you and for your group:

> "God, we want our lives to reflect the goodness and greatness of You and who You are! Show us how to do this in the big things and the little things of life. Help us see every opportunity as a way our lives can glorify You."

---

1. Billy Graham, in *Billy Graham in Quotes*, ed. Franklin Graham (Nashville: Thomas Nelson, 2011), 18.
2. Augustine, *The Confessions of St. Augustine: Modern English Version* (New York: Revell, 2005), 15-16.
3. Matt Chandler and Jared Wilson, *The Explicit Gospel* (Wheaton: Crossway, 2012), 104.
4. C.S. Lewis, *The Magician's Nephew* (New York: Macmillan Publishing Company, 1970), 99.
5. Millard J. Erickson, *Christian Theology* (Grand Rapids: Baker, 1998), 475.

> The angels' praise and service of God give us an example of how we are to conduct ourselves now and what our activity will be in the life beyond in God's presence.[5]
>
> **MILLARD J. ERICKSON**

NOTES

THE GOSPEL PROJECT

Session 2

The Enemy's Atrocity

Better to reign in Hell, than serve in Heaven.[1]
SATAN, IN *PARADISE LOST* BY JOHN MILTON

INDIVIDUAL STUDY

"The Force" from *Star Wars* has entered popular culture in a big way. It's become an informal way to think about the energy—for both good and evil—that holds everything together. In *Star Wars*, good guys (the Jedi) use the Force only for good, but bad guys (the Sith) use the dark side of the Force. If this were true, what would we make of the idea that evil has always been?

Think about how you would answer this question: "What is your belief about the origin of evil?" There are four major approaches here with very few variations in answering this question.

1. We can believe that there is no such thing as real evil—that it's only an illusion.

2. We can believe that evil has always coexisted alongside good, and that the universe has two eternal and opposing forces—like yin-yang in Taoism or the Force in *Star Wars*.

3. We can believe that there was only God (and good) in the beginning, but sometime before He created the earth God created evil as a thing lesser than Himself.

4. We can believe that evil is essentially not a "thing," but the absence of good. God created all things good but allowed His creatures to choose freely the non-good (evil).

All of these have been proposed by philosophies and religions through the ages. The fourth was laid out by the early church father Augustine in *Confessions* and *The City of God*. Many Christians through the centuries have found Augustine's view compelling.

> **If a child were to ask you, "Where did Satan come from?" and, "Why did God create Satan?" how would you respond? What should we do when the Bible doesn't give us all the answers we want about a particular topic?**

In this session, we see how God's good rule first came under attack. At some point after God created the world, Satan, one of God's angels, grew proud and rebelled against God's authority. In response, God cast Satan and the rebel angels out of His presence and promised one day to destroy them forever.

Throughout the week engage these daily study sections on your own. Each centers on a different aspect of Satan's rebellion. There are three daily readings to prepare you before your group meets. Interact with the Scriptures, and be ready to interact with your small group.

1 Satan was Created to Bring Glory to God

At the end of the creation account, we read that God saw all that He had made, and "it was very good" (Gen. 1:31). But in the account of humankind's fall into sin, we find a mysterious being present—"the serpent." Later this serpent is described as "the accuser" or "Satan." Through his cunning and questioning, the serpent led our first parents into sin.

The question before us now is, "Where did this mysterious being come from?" Since the Bible teaches that God created everything, we believe Satan himself began as part of God's creation of "the heavens." He was included in the heavenly host God created to praise Him (Ps. 148:1-2). He was probably among the angelic beings who "sang together" and "shouted for joy" when the earth was formed (Job 38:7). He was created to bring glory to God.

Bible scholars have inferred a timeline of Satan's existence:

1. God created all things.

2. As an angel, Satan was created before the earth was created.

3. As an angel, Satan probably glorified God at the earth's creation.

4. Everything, including Satan, was created good.

5. Sometime between Satan's creation and the garden of Eden scene (Gen. 3), Satan went from being good to being a tempter.

Ezekiel prophesied for some twenty years during the first part of the Jews' Babylonian captivity (around 593-571 B.C.). His stunning visions taught God's people about Yahweh's sovereign plan over them. Ezekiel spoke of God's present judgment on evil, but he also predicted remote future events in which God's kingdom would be expressed in righteousness.

> [11] The word of the LORD came to me: [12] "Son of man, lament for the king of Tyre and say to him: This is what the Lord GOD says: You were the seal of perfection, full of wisdom and perfect in beauty. [13] You were in Eden, the garden of God.

The Enemy's Atrocity

> Every kind of precious stone covered you: carnelian, topaz, and diamond,
> beryl, onyx, and jasper, sapphire, turquoise and emerald.
> Your mountings and settings were crafted in gold;
> they were prepared on the day you were created.
> [14] You were an anointed guardian cherub,
> for I had appointed you.
> You were on the holy mountain of God;
> you walked among the fiery stones.
> [15] From the day you were created
> you were blameless in your ways
> until wickedness was found in you.
> EZEKIEL 28:11-15

In Ezekiel's time, Tyre was a major seaport located on an island just off the coast of Phoenicia. This is modern-day Lebanon. It was wealthy, and its ruler was arrogant and self-sufficient. Ezekiel chapter 27 lamented Tyre as a city and prophesied its doom. Ezekiel chapter 28 turned attention from the city itself to its king. They refer primarily to the king of Tyre as a rebel against God. But not far below the surface, Bible scholars have long recognized that the king of Tyre was a human example of the first rebel against God—Satan. Note how the human king (as well as Satan) was created to bring glory to God:

- There was nothing lacking in wisdom or beauty (v. 12).

- There was nothing lacking in placement (v. 13). Tyre was in an ideal location in the Mediterranean. And of course, "Eden, the garden of God," is a reminder of the place in the biblical narrative where the serpent first appeared.

- There was nothing lacking in wealth and splendor (v. 13). The precious stones mentioned are a kaleidoscope of jewels, not all of which can be identified with certainty.

Why might it be easier for persons with abundant wisdom or beauty or wealth to be tempted to pride?

What gifts from God are we inclined to take credit for?

2 Satan Rebelled Against God

In addition to Ezekiel's portrait, many Bible scholars find an allusion to Satan behind the imagery of Isaiah 14. During the eighth century B.C. before Ezekiel's time, this great prophet brought a "Book of Judgment" (Isa. 1–39) against the idolatrous people of Judah and then a "Book of Comfort" (Isa. 40–66). Along the way Isaiah predicted the future downfall of the king of Babylon.

Just as Ezekiel's words first addressed the king of Tyre but also provide insight into Satan's situation, so Isaiah's words have application to Satan.

> 13 You said to yourself:
> "I will ascend to the heavens;
> I will set up my throne
> above the stars of God.
> I will sit on the mount of the gods' assembly,
> in the remotest parts of the North.
> 14 I will ascend above the highest clouds;
> I will make myself like the Most High."
> ISAIAH 14:13-14

Note that "I will" is repeated so aggressively. We see that the desire to challenge God as King—to seek to replace Him as Lord of the universe—is truly awful. Babylon's king thought he could set up an empire to rival God's.

Instead of humbling himself before God, he exalted himself. His desire was to remain in his lofty position. Only those full of pride would assert themselves to be "above the stars." He wanted to be like God.

> **In what ways do we mimic Satan every time we sin? What is the connection between idolatry and pride?**

Satan's pride led to his rebellion against the one and only true King of all things. This pride seems to have grown from his taking credit for qualities he wrongly assumed originated in himself. We can speculate that the descent of Satan went something like this.

1. God created Satan, bestowing on him wonderful qualities and abilities.

2. Satan began to take credit for what God had given him.

3. This pride led to a loss of wisdom.

4. Pride and a loss of wisdom led him to challenge God's rule and rebel.

This sequence is borne out when we return to Ezekiel. Again, the primary reference is to the king of Tyre, but we can see a double reference in how these words also apply to Satan. Here is what Yahweh proclaimed, recorded in Ezekiel 28:17-19:

> [17] Your heart became proud because of your beauty;
> For the sake of your splendor you corrupted your wisdom.
> So I threw you down to the earth; I made you a spectacle before kings.
> [18] You profaned your sanctuaries
> by the magnitude of your iniquities in your dishonest trade.
> So I made fire come from within you, and it consumed you.
> I reduced you to ashes on the ground in the sight of everyone watching you.
> [19] All those who know you among the nations are appalled at you.
> You have become an object of horror and will never exist again."

Verse 18 speaks of rebellion against God in terms of the king of Tyre/Satan having "profaned your sanctuaries," proceeding from "the magnitude of your iniquities." Small sins unchecked lead to great sins, which lead to great profanity against everything holy.

All human kings and kingdoms are fleeting. The most arrogant and seemingly invincible of empires have all crumbled into dust. Satan's demise, as we shall see, resulted in his being cast out of God's presence. He has not yet met his final doom. Ultimately, he and all his workers and works will be "thrown into the lake of fire and sulfur ... tormented day and night forever and ever" (Rev. 20:10).

> **In what ways do you personally combat pride? What are the things that remind us that the powers of this world are fleeting?**

3 Satan was Cast Out of God's Presence

What is a great and wonderful king to do when he finds a rebel among his subjects? Our inborn sense of justice cries out for the king to deal with the evil in his midst. Our eternal God is perfectly righteous and holy. He doesn't tolerate sin in His presence. So God had no choice but to cast out Satan from His presence.

Some Bible scholars believe the following words from John in the Book of Revelation apply to the initial rebellion:

> 7 Then war broke out in heaven: Michael and his angels fought against the dragon. The dragon and his angels also fought, 8 but he could not prevail, and there was no place for them in heaven any longer. 9 So the great dragon was thrown out—the ancient serpent, who is called the Devil and Satan, the one who deceives the whole world. He was thrown to earth, and his angels with him.
> **REVELATION 12:7-9**

Just imagine it—war broke out in heaven, the very heavens that were the first object of God's loving plan. And somehow in God's plan, He permitted Satan to roam the earth deceiving humanity and opposing Him. Ezekiel describes this kind of expulsion from the heavenly places:

> Through the abundance of your trade,
> you were filled with violence, and you sinned.
> So I expelled you in disgrace from the mountain of God,
> and banished you, guardian cherub,
> from among the fiery stones.
> **EZEKIEL 28:16**

The verbs *expelled* and *banished* are strong, and Isaiah helps us further understand the judgment that fell on Satan.

> [12] Shining morning star,
> how you have fallen from the heavens!
> You destroyer of nations,
> you have been cut down to the ground ...
> [15] But you will be brought down to Sheol
> into the deepest regions of the Pit.
> ISAIAH 14:12,15

This passage implies a two-stage judgment process. The first part of the judgment was to be cast from the heavens and therefore "cut down to the ground." The second step in the divine judgment was to be brought down from the earth to "Sheol," or "the deepest regions of the Pit."

How have you personally experienced God's correction against your pride?

Did you sense this more as discipline or mercy in action?

How does the coming final judgment against Satan and sin make us bolder in our mission to the lost to proclaim the King of God's kingdom?

Longing for the King

GROUP STUDY

Warm Up

Throughout the ages, theologians and poets have pondered what may have happened to lead Satan down the path from pride to rebellion. In English literature, there's nothing more profoundly suggestive as Milton's *Paradise Lost*. This poem depicts the pattern of revolt against God—both by Satan and his hosts as well as our first parents.

Before Milton, the ancient Greek philosophers understood the danger of pride. They referred to it as *hubris*—the overconfidence one has in their own abilities. Before that, Israel's Book of Proverbs had warned, "Pride comes before destruction, and an arrogant spirit before a fall" (Prov. 16:18).

In the New Testament, we find several truths about the Enemy. Focus on these Scriptures as you begin your small group discussion together.

- In the Old Testament, Satan is the tempter of humanity and the accuser. Jesus noted that he was "a murderer from the beginning" and "a liar and the father of liars" (John 8:44).

- One reason for Jesus' incarnation, life, death, and resurrection was to further judge Satan. He "was revealed for this purpose: to destroy the Devil's works" (1 John 3:8).

- Jesus' death was the decisive blow against Satan and his forces. God "disarmed the rulers and authorities and disgraced them publicly; He triumphed over them by [Jesus]" (Col. 2:15).

- Satan and his forces are still potent antagonists against believers. "Your adversary the Devil is prowling around like a roaring lion, looking for anyone he can devour" (1 Pet. 5:8).

- Believers equipped with the armor of God need not fear the Devil. We can "stand against the tactics of the Devil" (Eph. 6:11).

Describe common occasions and circumstances when we fight against pride. How can we take that opportunity to point others to God?

Discussion

The Bible doesn't answer all our questions about Satan. We don't know why God allows Satan a measure of freedom between the time he was cast from heaven and the time he will be cast into hell forever. But from this study of the Scriptures, we can walk away with a personal challenge. We should examine our own hearts to identify any pride which is taking credit for what God has done.

During this time you'll have an opportunity to discuss what God revealed to you during the week. Listed below are some of the questions from your daily reading assignments. They will guide your small-group discussion.

1. If a child were to ask you, "Where did Satan come from?" and, "Why did God create Satan?" how would you respond? What should we do when the Bible doesn't give us all the answers we want about a particular topic?

2. What gifts from God are we humans inclined to take credit for?

3. In what ways do we mimic Satan every time we sin? What is the connection between idolatry and pride?

4. In what ways do you personally combat pride? What are the things that remind us that the powers of this world are fleeting?

5. How have you personally experienced God's correction against your pride? Did you sense this more as discipline or mercy in action?

6. How does the coming final judgment against Satan and sin make us bolder in our mission to the lost to proclaim the King of God's kingdom?

Conclusion

God has never been thwarted by Satan's evil schemes. Before God even created the heavens or Satan himself, God planned to interpose Himself as the solution. God's plan to bring salvation was devised "before the foundation of the world" (Eph. 1:4). The result is that "at the name of Jesus every knee will bow ... and every tongue should confess that Jesus Christ is Lord" (Phil. 2:10-11). Satan's puny revolt against heaven will, in God's good time, give way to the final triumph of God's beloved Son, the King of kings and Lord of lords (Rev. 19–22).

> [5] Make your own attitude that of Christ Jesus, [6] who, existing in the form of God, did not consider equality with God as something to be used for His own advantage. [7] Instead He emptied Himself by assuming the form of a slave, taking on the likeness of men. And when He had come as a man in His external form, [8] He humbled Himself by becoming obedient to the point of death—even to death on a cross.
> **PHILIPPIANS 2:5-8**

Spend some time praying this for you and for your group:

> "God, we want to empty ourselves of all our sin and pride. Give us the wisdom and power to be more like Jesus. Help us to find contentment and joy from humbly following You."

---

1. John Milton, *Paradise Lost* (New York: Oxford University Press, reissue 2008), 11.
2. John of Damascus, *Exposition of the Orthodox Faith*, in *Nicene and Post-Nicene Fathers, Second Series*, vol. 9, eds. Philip Schaff and Henry Wace (Peabody, MA: Hendrickson, 1899, reprinted 2004), 20.

> [The Devil] was not made wicked in nature but was good, and made for good ends, and received from his Creator no trace whatever of evil in himself. But he did not sustain the brightness and the honour which the Creator had bestowed on him, and of his free choice was changed from what was in harmony to what was at variance with his nature ... and determined to rise in rebellion against [God].[2]
>
> **JOHN OF DAMASCUS (CIRCA 650-750)**

NOTES

THE GOSPEL PROJECT

Session 3

Our Identity

> We all long for [Eden], and we are constantly glimpsing it: our whole nature at its best and least corrupted, its gentlest and most human, is still soaked with the sense of "exile."
>
> **J. R. R. TOLKIEN**

INDIVIDUAL STUDY

Once upon a time, there was a handsome prince. He married the most beautiful girl in the kingdom. After two years, the prince's wife gave birth to a son who would one day become king. The royal family waved to adoring subjects as they traveled to the palace where they would raise their son and serve the monarch. And they lived happily ever after ...

Many fairy tales begin and end like this. Yet this story has recently played out in real life. On July 22, 2013, the Duchess of Cambridge (formerly Kate Middleton) gave birth to George Alexander Louis, Prince of Cambridge. The baby's father, Prince William, drove his family in a luxury automobile to London's Kensington Palace the next day. The royal couple with their newborn baby prince will one day sit on the British throne.

What about living "happily ever after"? In the real world, "happily ever after" is a lot harder to come by. Even fairy tales have conflict. This royal family has already experienced their own personal tragedy. Prince William lost his mother, Princess Diana, in a fiery car crash in Paris in 1997. And the royal family has been rocked with social scandals. Who knows what other difficulties are ahead for this young family?

> **What images do the words "once upon a time" bring to mind? What does "happily ever after" look like to you?**

This session focuses our attention on the original royal family—Adam and Eve. In the beginning, they were God's people living in God's place under God's loving rule. Eventually, something happened to disrupt this beautiful setting. We will see that God's good purpose all along has been for people to live in His world under His loving rule.

Throughout the week engage these daily study sections on your own. Each of them centers on a different aspect of our identity in God. There are three daily readings to prepare you before your group meets for this session. Interact with the Scriptures, and be ready to interact with your small group.

Longing for the King

1 God's Royal Place

Our recent study of Psalm 148 showed that God created the heavens first, and then the heavenly creatures praised Him. Next, God created the earth, and as the King, He designed earthly creatures to honor Him as their Creator. The creation account is famously told in Genesis 1. Then, like a movie scene that zooms in on the most important part of the action, the inspired writer described the creation of humankind and the home in which the people were placed (Gen. 1:26–2:25). Here's the way Genesis 2:8-15 describes that place—the garden of Eden:

> [8] The LORD God planted a garden in Eden, in the east, and there He placed the man He had formed. [9] The LORD God caused to grow out of the ground every tree pleasing in appearance and good for food, including the tree of life in the middle of the garden, as well as the tree of the knowledge of good and evil. [10] A river went out from Eden to water the garden. From there it divided and became the source of four rivers. [11] The name of the first is Pishon, which flows through the entire land of Havilah, where there is gold. [12] Gold from that land is pure; bdellium and onyx are also there. [13] The name of the second river is Gihon, which flows through the entire land of Cush. [14] The name of the third river is the Tigris, which runs east of Assyria. And the fourth river is the Euphrates. [15] The LORD God took the man and placed him in the garden of Eden to work it and watch over it.

Well-meaning Bible scholars have tried for centuries to pinpoint the geographical location of Eden. After all, the Tigris and Euphrates rivers were well known to early civilizations as part of the Fertile Crescent. But the Pishon and Gihon rivers could never be identified, nor could the land of Havilah. Perhaps it is best to conclude that our ability to identify the exact location of Eden vanished beneath the waters of the flood (see Gen. 6–8). We will receive greater benefit by looking at the other descriptions of Eden in the biblical account of God the King preparing a perfect place for the human beings created in His image to live.

The whole earth was "very good" when God finished His creative work. Thus, for Him to add to it a garden with every tree pleasing in appearance and good for food means that this was a perfect paradise indeed. There was abundance, more than enough for the human couple. Everything they could possibly need was provided. And what's more, God created humanity with the ability and desire to make useful and beautiful things. God meant for people to create culture—artifacts showing that humans made in His image could make things as their Creator did. Thus, the Lord put wonderful raw materials within reach, including pure gold as well as bdellium, likely an aromatic gum, and onyx, a semiprecious stone (see v.12). Further, the garden itself was designed for human hands. God placed the man in the garden of Eden "to work it and watch over it" (v. 15). In other words, God's perfect place was designed for the human touch.

> What is the most perfect place you've encountered? Why did you like it so much?

If the things we create say something about us, what does the planting of the Garden of Eden say about God? First, God is faithful. A compound form of God's name is used in Genesis 2. In English, *LORD God* represents the Hebrew *Yahweh Elohim*, that is, the covenant name of God in Israel (see Ex. 3:14-15) plus the term ordinarily translated *God* or *Deity*. For the ancient Israelites, there could be no question that when God created humanity and planted the garden, He was expressing His covenant faithfulness to the man and the woman.

Second, God expects obedience. God placed two special trees in the middle of the garden— "the tree of life" and "the tree of the knowledge of good and evil." There was nothing magical about these trees. God's intention in His loving rule was to give His people the opportunity to make morally meaningful choices. Obedience to God (choosing the tree of life) would result in blessing; disobedience (choosing the tree of the knowledge of good and evil) would result in death (see Gen. 2:17).

> Why do you think a longing for paradise is embedded in the hearts of men and women?

> What does this desire tell us about God's original design for humanity?

2 God's Royal People

How much attention have you given this question "How old is the universe?" or "How long ago did humankind first appear on the earth?" The center of biblical teaching about the origin of humankind—in both the Old and New Testaments—is that God created man and woman *in His image*, not *when* He actually created them. Consider these two passages from Genesis:

> ²⁷ So God created man in His own image;
> He created him in the image of God;
> He created them male and female.
> ²⁸ God blessed them, and God said to them, "Be fruitful, multiply, fill the earth, and subdue it. Rule the fish of the sea, the birds of the sky, and every creature that crawls on the earth." ²⁹ God also said, "Look, I have given you every seed-bearing plant on the surface of the entire earth and every tree whose fruit contains seed. This food will be for you, ³⁰ for all the wildlife of the earth, for every bird of the sky, and for every creature that crawls on the earth—everything having the breath of life in it. I have given every green plant for food." And it was so. ³¹ God saw all that He had made, and it was very good. Evening came and then morning: the sixth day.
> **GENESIS 1:27-31**

> ¹⁵ The LORD God took the man and placed him in the garden of Eden to work it and watch over it. ¹⁶ And the LORD God commanded the man, "You are free to eat from any tree of the garden, ¹⁷ but you must not eat from the tree of the knowledge of good and evil, for on the day you eat from it, you will certainly die."
> **GENESIS 2:15-17**

Theological discussions have pondered what it means that humanity alone was created in the image of God. Sometimes the explanation has revolved around the notion that God gave humans *personhood*—intellect, emotions, and will. Some have focused on the ancient custom of rulers setting up statues or images of themselves to show the reality of their reign in distant provinces. Still others have focused on the idea that an image is a representative as well as a representation.

The Genesis account shows that God subjected the lower earthly creation to the governance of humanity (see Gen. 1:28). For example, little dogs can't know God, but they can know their owners. In a representative sense, we dog owners are the image of God to our pets. We represent God to all non-human creatures.

Our Identity

While the debate over the meaning of the image of God continues, Scripture clearly teaches that the image-bearers of God's glory are people characterized by the following:

- Male and female best reflect God together. However badly the genders have treated each other, it's surely only when the two genders work together that the image of God is most fully expressed in us (1:27).

- Humanity is under the blessing of God to increase the human population. Someone has observed that "be fruitful and multiply" is the only command of God that human beings have ever completely and willingly obeyed (1:28)!

- Humankind is under the blessing of God to manage—"subdue" and "rule"—all earthly creatures, those in the sky and in the sea and on the earth, including plant life (1:28-29).

- Humanity's rule under God was to spread from Eden through the rest of the planet. In the command to "fill the earth," the people were to tend to and use every seed-bearing plant and tree on "the surface of the entire earth" (1:28-29).

> **How can recognizing the brokenness of earth through human sin and mismanagement point us back to the goodness of the Creator?**

> **How do you fulfill your responsibility as ruler over earth's creatures and resources?**

God placed Adam and Eve in a position to make moral decisions—choosing between good and evil. They were free to eat from any tree they chose (2:16), just as a king and queen might. But God set up a single decision as a test for the first royal couple. He warned that if they failed, there would be severe consequences. We can describe this situation in a very simple way—command and consequence. They were commanded, "Do not eat from the tree of the knowledge of good and evil." Here's the consequence: "If you do eat, you will certainly die on that day."

> **How is God's goodness seen in giving humankind the moral ability to obey or disobey Him?**

Longing for the King

3 God's Loving Rule

So far, we have seen God's royal place and His royal people. Now we turn to God's loving rule in creation as seen in Psalm 95. Verses 1-7 of this psalm could almost have been a song of Adam and Eve in the garden as they celebrated life under God's love and rule. Psalm 95 is clear in its call to worship the Creator God, who rules over His people with power and goodness:

> [1] Come, let us shout joyfully to the LORD,
> shout triumphantly to the rock of our salvation!
> [2] Let us enter His presence with thanksgiving;
> let us shout triumphantly to Him in song.
> [3] For the LORD is a great God,
> a great King above all gods.
> [4] The depths of the earth are in His hand,
> and the mountain peaks are His.
> [5] The sea is His; He made it.
> His hands formed the dry land.
> [6] Come, let us worship and bow down;
> let us kneel before the LORD our Maker.
> [7] For He is our God,
> and we are the people of His pasture,
> the sheep under His care.
> Today, if you hear His voice:
> [8] Do not harden your hearts as at Meribah,
> as on that day at Massah in the wilderness
> [9] where your fathers tested Me;
> they tried Me, though they had seen what I did.
> [10] For 40 years I was disgusted with that generation;
> I said, "They are a people whose hearts go astray;
> they do not know My ways."
> [11] So I swore in My anger,
> "They will not enter My rest."
> PSALM 95:1-11

Our Identity

First, we see *how* we are to praise God. Verses 1-2 tell us that praise is verbal—we are to shout triumphantly and sing with thanksgiving. Verse 6 shows us that praise involves our whole selves—to bow down and kneel in worship. Genuine praise to God includes our words and our literal posture.

Second, we see *why* we are to praise God. The exhortation of each part of Psalm 95 continues by extolling God's greatness. This "great King" is the Creator of all things—the depths of the earth, the mountain peaks in the sky, the sea, and the land. God created them all (vv. 3-5). "Our God" is also a loving Ruler for His people—shepherding and caring for the people of His pasture (v. 7).

How do you connect to God in worship?

Why do you participate in worship of the Creator God?

Though God's loving rule over creation has been evident from the beginning, the last few verses of Psalm 95 remind us that sin has indeed entered the world, and there have been terrible consequences. Adam and Eve in the garden couldn't have sensed the sorrow of these verses, but we most certainly can.

In God's royal place, access to the tree of life was barred once the royal couple had sinned. "He [and she] must not reach out, and also take from the tree of life, eat, and live forever" (Gen. 3:22). But this was not the end of God's loving rule. The story of the Bible from the curse forward to the new heavens and new earth is the story of the King's redeeming love. We live between the curse and the final reversal foretold in Revelation 22:2-3: "The tree of life was on both sides of the river ... and there will no longer be any curse." Then, indeed, we will experience perfectly God's people in God's place under God's loving rule.

In what ways does Jesus fulfill the reality of God's people, God's place, and God's rule?

Longing for the King

GROUP STUDY

Warm Up

Take a moment to read these quotes from world history, church leadership, and pop culture. Let them sink in as you begin your discussion.

> In the garden of Eden, we see the world as God designed it to be. God's people, Adam and Eve, live in God's place, the garden, under his rule as they submit to his word. And to be under God's rule in the Bible is always to enjoy his blessing; it is the best way to live. God's original creation shows us a model of his kingdom as it was meant to be.[2]
>
> **VAUGHAN ROBERTS**

> Initially, when I first became a Christian and got into ministry, my thought was that God existed to make my life better and to take me to heaven. Now I realize that it is not about me at all. It is all about God and that He did this to display His plan to restore the Earth to the Garden of Eden state.[3]
>
> **MAX LUCADO**

> God is the Ruler of His mighty creation. There is no reason to despair, because He holds in His hands the whole world, while His Spirit is able to fill the void in man's heart.[4]
>
> **BILLY GRAHAM**

How has the acceptance or rejection of the creation story affected culture?

To what degree do you think Genesis 1–3 shapes our foundational beliefs about God and humanity? Explain your answer.

How can we tap into the universal desire for a "perfect world" shared by all of humanity to further the conversation about Jesus Christ?

Discussion

In the ESV Study Bible, T. Desmond Alexander submits a wonderful explanation of the ancient Hebrew understanding of the garden of Eden. This couldn't be a more perfect notion as you begin your small group discussion.

> The name "Eden," which would have conveyed the sense of "luxury, pleasure," probably denotes a region much greater than the garden itself. God formed the man in the "land," and then put him in the garden. The earliest translation into Greek (the Septuagint) used the word *paradeisos* (from which comes the English term 'paradise' ...) to translate the Hebrew term for "garden," on the understanding that it resembled a royal park.[5]

T. DESMOND ALEXANDER

During this time you will have an opportunity to discuss what God revealed to you during the week. Listed below are some of the questions from your daily reading assignments. They will guide your small-group discussion.

1. What images do the words "once upon a time" bring to mind? What does "happily ever after" look like to you?

2. What is the most perfect place you've encountered? Why did you like it so much?

3. Why do you think a longing for paradise is embedded in the hearts of men and women? What does this desire tell us about God's original design for humanity?

4. How can recognizing the brokenness of earth through human sin and mismanagement point us back to the goodness of the Creator?

5. How is God's goodness seen in giving humankind the moral ability to obey or disobey Him?

6. In what ways does Jesus fulfill the reality of God's people, God's place, and God's rule?

Conclusion

The ideal of "once upon a time" in human history came to a crashing end in the garden of Eden. But that didn't put an end to God's plan for His kingdom on earth. Human kings and kingdoms come and go, but there still awaits for us an eternal "happily ever after." There is One who will rule His Father's throne forever and ever. Jesus came for the express purpose of moving the story of God's kingdom forward.

His first message after His baptism was "The time is fulfilled, and the kingdom of God has come near" (Mark 1:15). As the King of God's kingdom, He has established the church. Believers are already the people of God and comprise the temple of God under the rule of the Christ of God (1 Pet. 2:5,10,21). Our purpose is to point people to the Christ that they too may "glorify God on the day of visitation" (1 Pet. 2:12).

Spend some time praying this for you and for your group:

> "God, we want to find our identity in You! Teach us how to see ourselves as You see us. Lead us down the path of obedience in Your place and under Your love, and help us to express 'who we are' and 'Whose we are' to those who need You."

---

1. J. R. R. Tolkien, in *The Letters of J. R. R Tolkien*, ed. Humphrey Carpenter (Boston: Houghton Mifflin, 2000), 110.
2. Vaughan Roberts, *God's Big Picture* (Downers Grove: IVP, 2002), 23.
3. Michelle A. Vu, interview with Max Lucado. *The Christian Post*. 05 October 2011. Accessed 11 April 2014. *Online at* http://www.christianpost.com/news/interview-max-lucado-on-storytelling-the-church-and-politics-57347/
4. Billy Graham, in *Billy Graham in Quotes*, ed. Franklin Graham (Nashville: Thomas Nelson, 2011), 89.
5. T. Desmond Alexander, Genesis footnote 2:8-9 in the *ESV Study Bible*, ed. Lane T. Dennis, (Wheaton: Crossway Bibles, 2008), 53.
6. Martin Luther, *Lectures on Genesis*, 2:9, in *Genesis 1–11*, ed. John L. Thompson, vol. I in *Reformation Commentary on Scripture: Old Testament* (Downers Grove: IVP, 2012), 80.

> This tree of the knowledge of good and evil was Adam's church, altar, and pulpit. Here he was to yield to God the obedience he owed, give recognition to the Word and will of God, give thanks to God, and call upon God for aid against temptation… Therefore let us learn that some external form of worship and a definite work of obedience were necessary for man, who was created to have all the other living creatures under his control, to know his Creator, and to thank Him.[6]
>
> **MARTIN LUTHER**

NOTES

THE GOSPEL PROJECT

Session 4

Altered Humanity

It is when man through selfish ambition seeks to be God in his own life and will that he sins. Sin is dethroning God and enthroning self.[1]

HERSCHEL HOBBS (1907-1995)

Altered Humanity

INDIVIDUAL STUDY

A raised, clenched fist. It's become a universal symbol of rebellion against the status quo. Recall the political rebellions you've heard about or witnessed on television. For example, in 2011, the Arab Spring launched revolutions in a number of Arab countries, forcing many rulers from power. A bit further back were the Revolutions of 1989, overthrowing communist dictatorships in Central and Eastern Europe. Even the once-mighty USSR dissolved in 1991.

Although we usually think of rebellions in a military or political sense, there are rebellions of other kinds as well. Teenagers rebel against their parents. In the 1960s, an entire generation who believed in "free love, drugs, and rock-n-roll" rebelled against the cultural norms embraced by the establishment.

There are religious rebellions, too. The Protestant Reformation of the 16th century was very much a religious rebellion against the authority of the papacy. Martin Luther, in essence, raised his fist against the injustice (and religious errors) that he perceived in his day. Even today, the term *Protestant* includes the notion of protest.

The earliest unjustified rebellion occurred at the beginning of human history—the revolt of Adam and Eve against their righteous, loving God. Our first parents raised their fists against Him, and their descendants have proven to be like their ancestors. We too live as rebels against God, until He graciously overcomes our hostility against Him.

> What examples of rebellion—just or unjust—have you witnessed? When have you ever participated openly in an act of rebellion?

In this session, we'll see how paradise is lost when human beings rebel against God. Because of their rejection of God's good rule, the first humans were exiled from the garden of Eden. The good relationship between the King, His people, and the rest of creation was thrown into turmoil because of Adam and Eve's act of rebellion. But God promised to reestablish His kingdom through a future King who will undo the curse that came as a result of sin.

Throughout the week engage these daily study sections on your own. Each of them centers on a different aspect of how sin altered the state of humanity. There are three daily readings to prepare you before your group meets for this session. Interact with the Scriptures, and be ready to interact with your small group.

Longing for the King

The Royal Couple Refuses God's Rule

In the previous session, we saw God's people in God's place under God's loving rule. The Genesis account of the fall of humanity into sin is terse. It doesn't answer all our questions, but it gives us enough to know that Adam and Eve brought guilt and shame on themselves because of their willful disobedience against God. Here's the account in Genesis 3:

> ¹ Now the serpent was the most cunning of all the wild animals that the LORD God had made. He said to the woman, "Did God really say, 'You can't eat from any tree in the garden'?" ² The woman said to the serpent, "We may eat the fruit from the trees in the garden. ³ But about the fruit of the tree in the middle of the garden, God said, 'You must not eat it or touch it, or you will die.'" ⁴ "No! You will not die," the serpent said to the woman. ⁵ "In fact, God knows that when you eat it your eyes will be opened and you will be like God, knowing good and evil." ⁶ Then the woman saw that the tree was good for food and delightful to look at, and that it was desirable for obtaining wisdom. So she took some of its fruit and ate it; she also gave some to her husband, who was with her, and he ate it.
> GENESIS 3:1-6

Let's look at how this scene played out. Notice the progression:

THE SERPENT'S INITIAL QUESTION TO EVE. Genesis is silent as to how the serpent allowed Satan access to the garden. We are neither told if Eve was surprised by a talking animal nor why Adam was silent. We know that Adam was present (see v. 6). The serpent's question was to cause doubt about what God's word and intention had been. The serpent's question implied God was being harsh.

EVE'S DISTORTION OF GOD'S WORD. Eve had it partially right. God had commanded them not to eat fruit from one particular tree: "You are free to eat from any tree of the garden, but you must not eat from the tree of the knowledge of good and evil, for on the day you eat from it, you will certainly die" (Gen. 2:16-17). But God never said anything about touching the fruit.

Altered Humanity

How did the serpent twist the idea that God is good and loving? How do you see the Enemy continue to do this today?

THE SERPENT'S DENIAL OF GOD'S WORD. Next, the serpent flat out contradicted God, and the woman should have fled its presence at that point. "You will not die," was a huge lie indeed, and every human death proves the serpent was a liar. The pattern now has been set, and the results will be inescapable. Questioning God's Word can lead to distorting God's Word, which in turn can lead to denial of His Word.

THE SERPENT'S IMPUGNING OF GOD'S MOTIVES. What reason could the woman have had to suppose that God was withholding something good from her? Where does that kind of thought come from, especially within the context of Eden—God's royal park? How could she possibly think that knowing evil—by personal experience—was desirable? The serpent's biggest hook was the falsehood, "You will be like God." In many ways, that is the essence of every sin—we want to be little gods rather than submit to the one true God. Sadly, Satan's lie worked the first time, and he has enjoyed limitless success with the same lie ever since.

In what ways have you "raised your fist" against God?

How do you keep from believing the Enemy's lies about God? What is essential for keeping a guard over your mind and heart against the onslaught of his attacks?

Longing for the King

2 The Royal Couple's Broken Relationship

The passage immediately following the temptation and the fall is highly suggestive of the way sin splits person from self, person from person, and person from God. Look at Genesis 3:7-13:

> 7 Then the eyes of both of them were opened, and they knew they were naked; so they sewed fig leaves together and made loincloths for themselves. 8 Then the man and his wife heard the sound of the LORD God walking in the garden at the time of the evening breeze, and they hid themselves from the LORD God among the trees of the garden. 9 So the LORD God called out to the man and said to him, "Where are you?" 10 And he said, "I heard You in the garden and I was afraid because I was naked, so I hid." 11 Then He asked, "Who told you that you were naked? Did you eat from the tree that I commanded you not to eat from?" 12 Then the man replied, "The woman You gave to be with me—she gave me some fruit from the tree, and I ate." 13 So the LORD God asked the woman, "What is this you have done?" And the woman said, "It was the serpent. He deceived me, and I ate."

Note first how sin results in personal dysfunction. Previously, "both the man and his wife were naked, yet felt no shame" (Gen. 2:25). But once they rebelled, shame entered their awareness. They instantly tried to remedy this situation with fig-leaf, but they couldn't cover themselves from God or from each other.

Adam also experienced fear for the first time: "I heard You in the garden and I was afraid because I was naked" (v. 10). This suggests an awareness of personal guilt. Shame and guilt had entered the world of humanity, and we have all suffered the same from these evil twins.

Why is this story of rebellion important for understanding all of Scripture?

Adam was quick to blame both God and Eve for what had happened: "The woman You gave to be with me." Eve fired back: "It was the serpent." Here's the first blame game in human history, and we've all learned to play the game. When we're personally threatened, we shift responsibility from ourselves.

Altered Humanity

Now, most importantly, watch how sin results in a broken relationship with God. We saw in Adam and Eve's rebellion a choice to follow a creature's wishes rather than the Creator's command (3:6). This choice led to an unraveling of their relationship with God. Whatever else their shame and guilt involved, it was treason against the King. Their first attempt at hiding from God was a pathetic fig-leaf garment. Their second attempt was to run and hide from God when He approached them. Their third attempt was to shift blame to others.

> Have you ever witnessed or experienced this kind of relationship? Describe how relational harmony can be destroyed by selfishness.

God unveiled His character by asking hard questions. He also asked questions to reveal just how far the humans had strayed. For each question, God knew the answer. He used the following questions both to display His righteousness and to get His children to acknowledge their sin.

"WHERE ARE YOU?" God's main concern was where they were literally, not spiritually. He was prompting them to make them think about where their relationship was with Him.

"WHO TOLD YOU THAT YOU WERE NAKED?" Adam had no answer. For us, the question might be paraphrased, "How did you come to know you're without?" As we diagnose our own sins, we need to be sure we are basing our insights on God and His Word alone.

"DID YOU EAT FROM THE TREE THAT I COMMANDED YOU NOT TO EAT FROM?" God wanted him to admit his sinful action, but Adam played the blame game.

"WHAT IS THIS YOU HAVE DONE?" This is the only question directed to Eve. Like the previous question, it was meant to prompt confession of sin. And Eve too admitted her sin.

Adam and Eve's story is historical, and it's also the story of every human. We all know that rebellion against the true King has broken our relationship with Him. We, like Adam and Eve, hide from God as well as from each other.

> What kinds of questions has God been asking you?

Longing for the King

3 God Exiles the Royal Couple

The rest of Genesis 3 declares God's curse on the serpent, the woman, and the man. Then they're banished from the garden. Yet a note of hope is included amid the judgment—God promises the coming of the seed (descendant) of the woman, who will crush the serpent.

> [14] Then the LORD God said to the serpent:
> Because you have done this,
> you are cursed more than any livestock
> and more than any wild animal.
> You will move on your belly
> and eat dust all the days of your life.
> [15] I will put hostility between you and the woman,
> and between your seed and her seed.
> He will strike your head,
> and you will strike his heel.
> [16] He said to the woman:
> I will intensify your labor pains;
> you will bear children in anguish.
> Your desire will be for your husband,
> yet he will rule over you.
> [17] And He said to Adam, "Because you listened to your wife's voice and ate from the tree about which I commanded you, 'Do not eat from it':
> The ground is cursed because of you.
> You will eat from it by means of painful labor
> all the days of your life.
> [18] It will produce thorns and thistles for you,
> and you will eat the plants of the field.
> [19] You will eat bread by the sweat of your brow
> until you return to the ground,
> since you were taken from it.
> For you are dust,
> and you will return to dust."
>
> **GENESIS 3:14-19**

THE SERPENT'S CURSE. The serpent was "the most cunning of all the wild animals" (Gen. 3:1); now God declared it "cursed ... more than any wild animal." Verse 14 is a curse on this specific beast rather than on all snakes or reptiles. In verse 15, however, the reference is not to a wild animal but a specific future judgment against Satan. Satan would continue for a season to inflict his poison: "you will strike his heel." But in the end, a descendant of the woman would "strike [Satan's] head." The judgment on Satan would result in his final demise; the judgment on humanity, however, would play out differently.

THE WOMAN'S CURSE. Eve and all women within humanity were judged by God. The female role as a mother begins with painful labor and delivery. Her role as a wife will be difficult. Whereas Adam and Eve had previously enjoyed perfect relational harmony, now there would be ongoing stress. Marriage won't be easy. Rather than rule over the earth together, each spouse will try to rule and dominate over the other. Sin damages marriage.

THE MAN'S CURSE. Work had been God's intention for humankind before sin entered the world (see Gen. 2:15). The rule over the earth that God had given to humanity was now damaged. Now work would be painful labor. Instead of a pleasant garden with fruit trees to tend, Adam would find uncooperative ground full of weeds and thorns. Instead of being fulfilled, Adam would be exhausted after a day's work.

> What are some current examples that show God's judgment on sin?

God had pronounced judgment on the serpent, the woman, and the man. But thankfully, in this judgment account, there was mercy. God didn't strike Adam and Eve dead that day. Instead of killing them, He killed animals in their place, so they wouldn't have to physically do without. God did banish our first parents from access to the tree of life, but He didn't destroy the tree; for He knew that one day the tree of life would become available to the sons and daughters of Adam and Eve once again.

> What happens when we fail to understand the seriousness of sin in our lives and its implications for our mission?

Longing for the King

GROUP STUDY

Warm Up

Read the Temptation of Jesus in Matthew 4:1-11 and then Adam and Eve's encounter with temptation in Genesis 3:14-19. Notice that Satan's playbook really hasn't changed all that much. What makes the difference is how we respond. Discuss the following observations.

	The Original Temptation	**Jesus' Temptation**
The person tempted	Eve, the first woman	Jesus, the last Adam
The place of temptation	Eden, a perfect garden	The wilderness of Judea
The temptation of the eyes	The fruit was beautiful	The kingdoms were glorious
The temptation of the appetite	The fruit was delicious	Stones could become bread
The temptation of the reputation	She would become wise	He could leap unharmed
The response	Human Reasoning	God's Word: "It is written …"
The result of temptation	Succumbed: sin and death	Resisted: obedience to God

What other similarities or differences do you see?

How is our mission in the world connected to the story of Adam and Eve's sin?

Discussion

We see in Adam and Eve's eating of the forbidden fruit a betrayal of the true King and choosing another—a false king. In their betrayal, they lost their own place in God's kingdom as royal subjects under Him. Adam forfeited many aspects of his reign. Satan gained a measure of rule over the affairs of humankind. "The god of this age has blinded the minds of the unbelievers so they cannot see the light of the gospel" (2 Cor. 4:4).

During this time you will have an opportunity to discuss what God revealed to you during the week. Listed below are some of the questions from your daily reading assignments. They will guide your small-group discussion.

1. When have you ever participated openly in an act of rebellion? In what ways have you "raised your fist" against God?

2. How did the serpent twist the idea that God is good and loving? How do you see the Enemy continue to do this today?

3. Why do you think this story of rebellion against God so important for understanding the rest of the Bible?

4. What are some ways practical ways our sin has resulted in relational dysfunction?

5. Chronicle any warning signs that your relationship with God has been broken. What areas need to be confessed and forgiven?

6. Why must we recognize God as the Judge who does what is right (even when this means punishment on people)?

7. Think about how Genesis 3 serve as an introduction to the rest of the Bible. How do the last verses in Genesis 3 give us hope? How do they give you hope?

Conclusion

Adam and Eve raised their fists in rebellion against their true King. As a result, paradise was lost. Because of their rejection of God's good rule, the first humans were exiled from the garden of Eden. All their perfect relationships were turned into turmoil—their relationship with their King, their relationship with each other, and their relationship with the rest of creation. All of it was spoiled.

However, even as God cursed the serpent, the woman, the man, and the ground, He promised to reestablish His kingdom. There would come a time when a King would undo the curse that came as a result of sin. This promise points the way forward to the rest of the biblical story line. Abraham and Sarah, Moses and the Exodus, David and his coming Son—these are the stories of God's kingdom moving forward toward its final expression. This story is our story. And the story continues in and through what God is doing in us today.

Spend some time praying this for you and for your group:

> "God, we admit that our lives don't reflect You all of the time. Show us how to resist the Enemy and claim victory in the mighty name of King Jesus. We surrender our lives to You. Do Your work of restoration and hope and love in our hearts."

---

1. Herschel Hobbs, *The Baptist Faith and Message* (Nashville: Convention Press, 1971, revised 1996), 45.
2. Dirk Philips, *Concerning Spiritual Restitution*, in *Early Anabaptist Spirituality: Selected Writings*, trans. and ed. Daniel Liechty, 221.

> Because human beings did not remain in this original state of creation and lost the image of God through their disobedience, human beings had to be recreated by God through Jesus Christ. That is why the son of God was promised to Adam. This son appeared to all people and destroyed the work of the devil.[2]
>
> **DIRK PHILIPS (1504-1568)**

NOTES

THE GOSPEL PROJECT

Session 5

Stuck In Mediocrity

Authority to be lasting must be of the same order as that of Jesus Christ, not the authority of autocracy or coercion, but the authority of worth, to which all that is worthy in a man bows down. It is only the unworthy in a man that does not bow down to worthy authority.[1]

OSWALD CHAMBERS

INDIVIDUAL STUDY

A nuclear war has broken out. While the rest of the world is in chaos, a group of well-educated, well-behaved English schoolboys crash into the paradise of a deserted island with no adult survivors. Do you know what happens next?

In 1954, William Golding graphically played out this scenario in his book *Lord of the Flies*. Instead of creating a new society of harmony and peace, these little boys fight for power, hunt and kill one another, and even cut off the head of a pig to make a sacrifice to an imaginary and yet utterly real beast on the island. Golding uses this beast as a symbol for the evil in the heart of every person, even children, and ultimately shows the consequences of what the world would look like if all rule and authority were removed or rejected.

Golding's book, selling more than 15 million copies, is popular not because it's so unbelievable but because it's so frighteningly possible. The underlying moral logic of this story is an imaginary outworking of the truth about the nature and condition of our own hearts. We are people who constantly reject God's rule and authority over our lives.

> **What other books or movies remind you of *Lord of the Flies?* Imagine a society without any authority or rule. Would this society be free? Explain.**

Moses once foretold the establishment of a king for Israel and described the kind of servant-king God intended to lead His people. But years later, the Israelites rejected God's kingship and their unique identity as His people by demanding a king for the purpose of making them like other nations. Saul, the first king, failed to live up to God's standard and the expectations of God's people. Like Israel, we look for deliverance in places other than God, and just as with Saul, these lesser saviors always disappoint, revealing our need for the true King from God.

Throughout the week engage these daily study sections on your own. Each of them centers on a different aspect of the unfulfilled and disappointed life we have without God. There are three daily readings to prepare you before your group meets for this session. Interact with the Scriptures, and be ready to interact with your small group.

Longing for the King

God Desires an Obedient King

During the period of the judges, foreign nation after foreign nation invaded, killed, and put God's people under servitude. During these 400 years, other nations had kings who led their people and fought their battles. But Israel had no king. For this reason, the Israelites desperately wanted a king.

You might be familiar enough with the story to know that this was a sinful desire in God's eyes. But what made it so evil? It wasn't that they desired a king. In fact, God had always planned on providing a king for His people. In Deuteronomy 17:14-20, God spoke through Moses, saying:

> 14 "When you enter the land the LORD your God is giving you, take possession of it, live in it, and say, 'I will set a king over me like all the nations around me,' 15 you are to appoint over you the king the LORD your God chooses. Appoint a king from your brothers. You are not to set a foreigner over you, or one who is not of your people. 16 However, he must not acquire many horses for himself or send the people back to Egypt to acquire many horses, for the LORD has told you, 'You are never to go back that way again.' 17 He must not acquire many wives for himself so that his heart won't go astray. He must not acquire very large amounts of silver and gold for himself. 18 When he is seated on his royal throne, he is to write a copy of this instruction for himself on a scroll in the presence of the Levitical priests. 19 It is to remain with him, and he is to read from it all the days of his life, so that he may learn to fear the LORD his God, to observe all the words of this instruction, and to do these statutes. 20 Then his heart will not be exalted above his countrymen, he will not turn from this command to the right or the left, and he and his sons will continue ruling many years over Israel."
>
> **DEUTERONOMY 17:14-20**

God's king would be one of God's people and would understand the seduction of power, idolatry, and riches (vv. 15-17). He would recognize that he isn't supreme but is under God's authority. He would be a servant to God's people, not a tyrant over them (vv. 18-20).

When we encounter the Israelites in the Book of Judges, we can quickly conclude that the absence of a king leads us to do whatever we want. Without a king, the Israelites did what was right in their own eyes (see Judg. 21:25). This just led to an ongoing cycle of sin, judgment, and deliverance. God raised up deliverers who brought temporary peace, while at the same time revealing Israel's need for salvation.

> If you found $10 million, and you could do whatever you wanted with it, what would you do? Would you show restraint and discipline, or would you take a more liberal approach?

> What are some ways we're tempted to do what's right in our own eyes?

> What are the dangers of deciding for ourselves what's right for me or right for you?

Longing for the King

 # The People Demand a Conventional King

Fulfilling what God said would happen in Deuteronomy 17, the Israelites finally asked for a king in 1 Samuel 8:4-9:

> ⁴ So all the elders of Israel gathered together and went to Samuel at Ramah. ⁵ They said to him, "Look, you are old, and your sons do not follow your example. Therefore, appoint a king to judge us the same as all the other nations have." ⁶ When they said, "Give us a king to judge us," Samuel considered their demand sinful, so he prayed to the LORD. ⁷ But the LORD told him, "Listen to the people and everything they say to you. They have not rejected you; they have rejected Me as their king. ⁸ They are doing the same thing to you that they have done to Me, since the day I brought them out of Egypt until this day, abandoning Me and worshiping other gods. ⁹ Listen to them, but you must solemnly warn them and tell them about the rights of the king who will rule over them."
>
> 1 SAMUEL 8:4-9

God's sovereign plan included giving His people a king. So the Israelites' desire for a king wasn't particularly evil. But their words, clearly communicating their heart, showed this was no benign request. The Israelites wanted a king so they could be like all the other nations and because they didn't want God to be their King. They demanded a conventional king.

What are some good things we ask God for but with the wrong motivation? What might be a proper motivation for these requests?

We see that Israel's demand was a rejection of their uniqueness as the people of God (see 1 Sam. 8:5). God's people wanted to be like all the other nations. A chosen people—birthed and established by God, set apart, distinct, and holy—wanted to be like everybody else, as if God's children were junior high kids enamored by the latest fashion trend or cell phone.

Just think about how easy it is to "be the same" as everyone else. Though we're a chosen race, a royal priesthood, a holy nation (see 1 Pet. 2:9), many times we don't look that much different than anyone else.

How have you found yourself trying to be like everyone else?

SOCIALLY. We watch all the same TV shows and laugh at all the same jokes. Or perhaps we judge the Christians who do, not because we're genuinely concerned about their holiness but so we can socially fit into the group of "moral" people who refuse to do those things. Jesus was the most morally uncompromising person ever, and yet He ate with tax collectors and prostitutes and was called a friend of sinners.

ECONOMICALLY. Our standard of living increases as our salary increases. Making more money doesn't mean giving more but spending more. Or instead of spending it, we save, save, save. But we shouldn't fool ourselves. We're still spending that money, just to purchase for ourselves security and a good future. Jesus, though He was rich, for our sake became poor so that we, by His poverty, might become rich (see 2 Cor. 8:9).

PHYSICALLY. We either treat our bodies as worthless or we worship them. We can abuse our physical bodies with bad foods, no exercise, and sleeplessness thinking there won't be any spiritual consequences. Or we can tend to our bodies more than our souls. Jesus didn't have an impressive form or majesty that we should look upon Him; He had no appearance that we should desire Him (see Isa. 53:2). And yet the body that He had, He laid it down to be whipped, beaten, and hung on a cross.

SPIRITUALLY. We're just like most of the "polite" masses who never talk about politics or religion, and when we do talk about our faith, we use our "inside voice" so as not to offend anyone. Jesus' preaching got Him killed. He preached boldly, and people either followed Him or they wanted to kill Him.

In what specific ways can we follow Jesus' example socially, economically, physically, and spiritually?

What responses can we expect from those in the world when we follow His example?

Longing for the King

3 Israel's King Upsets God and the People

In 1 Samuel 9, we're introduced to Saul, an impressive young man, a head taller than all the other Israelites (9:2). In chapter 11, we see Saul lead the Israelites into battle and rescue them from the Ammonites. So this impressive young man showed promise, but how quickly things spiraled downward!

A centuries-old command from God had told the Israelites to completely annihilate the Amalekites (see Deut. 25:17-19). Why? The Amalekites were the first people the Israelites had to battle. You may think it was the Egyptians, but remember the Israelites never actually fought them. God delivered the Israelites from the Egyptian army as they stood silent and watched (see Ex. 14:13-14). Later, as God's people were on the way to Mount Sinai to receive God's law, the Amalekites attacked (17:8-15). They essentially tried to wipe out God's people before they even had a chance to learn to be God's people.

God reiterated this command through Samuel to Saul in 1 Samuel 15:1-3, and He made clear no one and no thing was to be spared destruction. But Saul didn't listen. He didn't completely destroy the Amalekites, for he kept the best sheep and cattle and took the Amalekite king as a prisoner instead of killing him as God had said (15:7-9). And when confronted about his disobedience (15:12-19), Saul made excuses:

> [20] "But I did obey the LORD!" Saul answered. "I went on the mission the LORD gave me: I brought back Agag, king of Amalek, and I completely destroyed the Amalekites. [21] The troops took sheep and cattle from the plunder—the best of what was set apart for destruction—to sacrifice to the LORD your God at Gilgal."
> [22] Then Samuel said:
> Does the LORD take pleasure in burnt offerings and sacrifices
>   as much as in obeying the LORD?
> Look: to obey is better than sacrifice,
>   to pay attention is better than the fat of rams.
> [23] For rebellion is like the sin of divination,
>   and defiance is like wickedness and idolatry.
> Because you have rejected the word of the LORD,
>   He has rejected you as king.

Stuck In Mediocrity

> ²⁴ Saul answered Samuel, "I have sinned. I have transgressed the Lord's command and your words. Because I was afraid of the people, I obeyed them. ²⁵ Now therefore, please forgive my sin and return with me so I can worship the Lord." ²⁶ Samuel replied to Saul, "I will not return with you. Because you rejected the word of the Lord, the Lord has rejected you from being king over Israel." ²⁷ When Samuel turned to go, Saul grabbed the hem of his robe, and it tore. ²⁸ Samuel said to him, "The Lord has torn the kingship of Israel away from you today and has given it to your neighbor who is better than you.
> 1 SAMUEL 15:20-28

When confronted by Samuel, Saul revealed himself to be a lesser king who disappoints: Saul claimed obedience (v. 20). Saul blamed others (v. 21). Saul tried to cover the wrong with something good—a sacrifice (v. 21). Saul admitted to being afraid of the people and wanting their approval more than God's (v. 24).

Was this the king God's people wanted? Yes. Was this the king God's people needed? Absolutely not. When we choose a king for ourselves, we find a lesser king who might give us what we want but can never give us what we need.

In what ways has God done this in your life—allowed you to have what you want instead of what you need?

How have you been disappointed by those in leadership positions?

Define a healthy attitude we should have toward those who lead, guide, and protect us.

Longing for the King

GROUP STUDY

Warm Up

Earlier in the week, we discussed the Israelites' desire for an earthly king. Read the rest of the story below from 1 Samuel 8:19-21. As God instructed, Samuel warned the people in verses 10-18 of all the ways this new king was going to look out for himself, and not the people. Saul would be a taker, not a giver, and the people would end up serving him rather than him serving the people. But the people responded:

> [19] The people refused to listen to Samuel. "No!" they said. "We must have a king over us. [20] Then we'll be like all the other nations: our king will judge us, go out before us, and fight our battles." [21] Samuel listened to all the people's words and then repeated them to the LORD.

God's people rejected Him as their King because (1) they wanted to be judged by the world's standards, and (2) they wanted to fight their own battles. But that's exactly what God did as their King.

> Where do you find yourself turning for fulfillment other than God?

> How do these "lesser kings" fail to deliver on their promise?

God is fighting for our hearts—the ultimate fight. And we need a King who will win the ultimate fight. All the lesser kings may lead us to places we think we want to go and win the things we think we want, but in the end they'll all disappoint. God's plan was always to win us over by offering His Son, Jesus Christ, the King of kings.

Discussion

During this time you'll have an opportunity to discuss what God revealed to you during the week. Questions from your daily reading assignments are listed below. They'll help guide your small-group discussion. But first, discuss this quote from John Piper. It describes how God is sovereign, even in the midst of our own poor choices. It communicates hope, because there's a God who sees the big picture, and He's ready and willing to work everything for our good if we let Him.

> The kingship of Israel—the fact that Israel had kings—was owing in part to sin. It was a spectacular sin for the people of God to say to their Maker and Redeemer, 'We want to be like the nations. We do not want you to be our king. We want a human king.' That is a spectacular sin. Samuel calls it ... a great wickedness. Nevertheless, if Israel had had no kingship, Jesus Christ would not have come as the king of Israel and the Son of David and King of kings. But Christ's kingship over Israel and over the world is not an afterthought in the mind of God. It was not an unplanned response to the sin of Israel. It was part of his plan.[2]
>
> **JOHN PIPER**

1. If you found $10 million, and you could do whatever you wanted with it, what would you do? Would you show restraint and discipline, or would you take a more liberal approach?

2. What are some ways we're tempted to do what's right in our own eyes?

3. What are the dangers of deciding for ourselves what's right for me or right for you?

4. What are some good things we ask God for but with the wrong motivation? What might be a proper motivation for these requests?

5. In what ways has God allowed you to have what you want instead of what you need?

6. How have you been disappointed by those in leadership positions?

7. Define a healthy attitude we should have toward those who lead, guide, and protect us.

Conclusion

King Saul was the first in a long line of lesser kings who displeased God and disappointed God's people. If the king we want falls so short, what kind of king, then, do we need? Instead of a lesser king claiming partial obedience, we need a King who fully obeys the Lord our God. Instead of blaming others, we need a King who bears our blame. Instead of covering up our wrongs with good things, such as a sacrifice, we need a King who sacrifices Himself for our wrongs. Instead of bowing to what the people want, we need a King who bows to what God wants and gives the people what they need.

Through the pathway of lesser king after lesser king, failed king after failed king, God would patiently lead the hearts of His people to long for the one true King—Jesus Christ, the King of kings. This King we may not want at times, but He's the King we and the world around us always need.

Spend some time praying this for you and for your group:

> "God, we don't want any other King to rule in our hearts except Jesus. We turn away from all those things we want, and we acknowledge the one thing we need. King Jesus, rule in our hearts today."

---

1. Oswald Chambers, in *The Quotable Oswald Chambers,* comp. and ed. David McCasland, 21.
2. John Piper, *Spectacular Sins* (Wheaton: CrossWay Books, 2008), 87.
3. Augustine, *Reply to Faustus the Manichean,* 22.67, quoted in *Nicene and Post-Nicene Fathers, First Series,* vol. 4, ed. Philip Schaff (Peabody, MA: Hendrickson, 1887, reprint 2004), 298.

> We must worship God from our inmost feelings, that out of the abundance of the heart the mouth may speak, instead of honoring Him with our lips, like the people of old, while our hearts are far from Him.[3]
>
> **AUGUSTINE (354-430)**

NOTES

THE GOSPEL PROJECT

Session 6

A Future Reality

"The text calls us not to admire David the man and no more, but to ponder what the Spirit of God may do with one person."[1]

D. A. CARSON

A Future Reality

INDIVIDUAL STUDY

Picture the scene. On the one hand, you've got an unknown, small-time boxer who works as a loan collector to make ends meet. His record is 44-20. On the other hand, you've got the heavy weight champion of the world with nicknames such as "The Dancing Destroyer," "The King of Sting," and "The Count of Monte Fisto." His record is 46-0 with 46 knockouts.

This was the setting for the 1976 film that won the Oscar for Best Picture—*Rocky*. Its budget was just over one million dollars. It was filmed in 28 days. So what was it about this movie that captured the hearts of so many people and brought in $225 million at the box office? It was the power of an "Underdog Story."

Whether it's a movie, a game, or an historic battle—we all love stories of underdogs overcoming great odds. But why do we find these stories so compelling? Why do they ring true? Perhaps it's because they faintly resemble the good news of salvation—how Christ went to the cross, was beaten, spat upon, and killed in our place, only to rise again, winning a triumphant victory through weakness. An Old Testament narrative that hints at and foreshadows the coming of this Savior is the famous story of David and Goliath.

> **What is the biggest underdog victory you've witnessed in sports or in business? What made it so memorable?**

We've discussed how the Israelites rejected God's kingship and their unique identity as His people. They demanded a king for the purpose of making them like other nations. Then we saw how Saul, the first king, failed to live up to God's standard and the expectations of God's people.

When God rejected Saul as king, He directed the prophet Samuel to anoint David, the son of Jesse. In the story of David, we see that God doesn't judge people based on worldly expectations. David's battle against Goliath is an example of a king's responsibility to fight for his people. In David, we see glimpses of the promised King we need as well as an example of obeying God from a heart on fire for Him.

Throughout the week engage these daily study sections on your own. Each of them centers on a different aspect of David's life—a picture of King Jesus. There are three daily readings to prepare you before your group meets for this session. Interact with the Scriptures, and be ready to interact with your small group.

Longing for the King

1 God's King vs. Worldly Expectations

¹ The LORD said to Samuel, "How long are you going to mourn for Saul, since I have rejected him as king over Israel? Fill your horn with oil and go. I am sending you to Jesse of Bethlehem because I have selected a king from his sons."
² Samuel asked, "How can I go? Saul will hear about it and kill me!"
The LORD answered, "Take a young cow with you and say, 'I have come to sacrifice to the LORD.' ³ Then invite Jesse to the sacrifice, and I will let you know what you are to do. You are to anoint for Me the one I indicate to you."
⁴ Samuel did what the LORD directed and went to Bethlehem. When the elders of the town met him, they trembled and asked, "Do you come in peace?"
⁵ "In peace," he replied. "I've come to sacrifice to the LORD. Consecrate yourselves and come with me to the sacrifice." Then he consecrated Jesse and his sons and invited them to the sacrifice. ⁶ When they arrived, Samuel saw Eliab and said, "Certainly the LORD's anointed one is here before Him."
⁷ But the LORD said to Samuel, "Do not look at his appearance or his stature, because I have rejected him. Man does not see what the LORD sees, for man sees what is visible, but the LORD sees the heart."
⁸ Jesse called Abinadab and presented him to Samuel. "The LORD hasn't chosen this one either," Samuel said. ⁹ Then Jesse presented Shammah, but Samuel said, "The LORD hasn't chosen this one either." ¹⁰ After Jesse presented seven of his sons to him, Samuel told Jesse, "The LORD hasn't chosen any of these." ¹¹ Samuel asked him, "Are these all the sons you have?"
"There is still the youngest," he answered, "but right now he's tending the sheep." Samuel told Jesse, "Send for him. We won't sit down to eat until he gets here." ¹² So Jesse sent for him. He had beautiful eyes and a healthy, handsome appearance.
Then the LORD said, "Anoint him, for he is the one." ¹³ So Samuel took the horn of oil, anointed him in the presence of his brothers, and the Spirit of the LORD took control of David from that day forward. Then Samuel set out and went to Ramah.
1 SAMUEL 16:1-13

The Lord directed Samuel to Bethlehem, to a man named Jesse and his sons. Samuel saw Eliab, the oldest son of Jesse and believed him to be the Lord's anointed, the next king of Israel. Most likely, Samuel came to this conclusion because of the appearance and stature of Eliab. "But the LORD said to him, 'Do not look at his appearance or his stature … Man does not see what the LORD sees, for man sees what is visible, but the LORD sees the heart'" (v. 7).

A Future Reality

We may think it was silly of Samuel to pick a king based solely upon height and stature, but in those days, it was the most natural thing to do. The height and stature of the king represented the height and stature of the nation. In those days, good kings went off to battle; they didn't just sit back in their palaces. Every nation and every army wanted to charge behind a king whom they could see above the heads of everyone else.

When Samuel was enamored by Eliab's physique, God told him that he was looking at the wrong thing. What's truly important isn't a man's stature but the character of his heart. God was pointing Samuel to the truth that physical looks, beauty, and attractiveness aren't ultimate. These are inconsequential and peripheral to what a person is on the inside. God showed Samuel the difference between a worldly perspective and a godly perspective that looks at the heart.

> **How do you judge those around you? In what ways are we enamored by the physical appearance of our leaders (political, spiritual, etc.)?**

> **How can you judge a person's heart (in a good way)? How do you get to know someone beyond the surface of physical appearance?**

The difference between worldly expectations and God's perspective on reality is relevant to us today. We live in a world where image is everything. We are bombarded by ads that feature images of women who don't look like anyone we know in real life or men who seem to be in perfect shape. The subtle message is that buying the product advertised will make you look or feel like the man or woman in the ad. The concern is for the outward appearance. But this isn't how God is. And this isn't how God wants us to see others.

> **In what ways does God's Word free us from judging ourselves based on appearances?**

Longing for the King

2 God's King Will Be Victorious

In the anointing of David as king, we saw how God's perspective is different than ours. In David's battle with Goliath, we see this principle on display again. From our perspective, we would never conclude victory for David, but again, that wouldn't be seeing things the way God sees them.

> ⁴⁵ David said to the Philistine: "You come against me with a dagger, spear, and sword, but I come against you in the name of Yahweh of Hosts, the God of Israel's armies—you have defied Him. ⁴⁶ Today, the LORD will hand you over to me. Today, I'll strike you down, cut your head off, and give the corpses of the Philistine camp to the birds of the sky and the creatures of the earth. Then all the world will know that Israel has a God, ⁴⁷ and this whole assembly will know that it is not by sword or by spear that the LORD saves, for the battle is the LORD's. He will hand you over to us."
> ⁴⁸ When the Philistine started forward to attack him, David ran quickly to the battle line to meet the Philistine. ⁴⁹ David put his hand in the bag, took out a stone, slung it, and hit the Philistine on his forehead. The stone sank into his forehead, and he fell on his face to the ground. ⁵⁰ David defeated the Philistine with a sling and a stone. Even though David had no sword, he struck down the Philistine and killed him. ⁵¹ David ran and stood over him. He grabbed the Philistine's sword, pulled it from its sheath, and used it to kill him. Then he cut off his head. When the Philistines saw that their hero was dead, they ran.
> 1 SAMUEL 17:45-51

Goliath of Gath was the Philistine champion. He stood nine feet and nine inches tall. Each day, he came out and stood on the edge of his hill and bellow insults to God's people. As he stood and screamed, the Israelites lost courage and were terrified. Their hearts melted like wax before this giant.

> **Why is it important that David waged a battle in the name of the Lord? What if he had come against Goliath in his own power?**

How does the Enemy try to intimidate you into giving up before the battle begins?

This story prepares the way for God to raise up another King who would accomplish another decisive victory—King Jesus who will come and slay the serpent and rescue people from sin and death.

In David, we see a picture of courageous faith in God's power. We also catch a glimpse of the bigger story of the Bible—the coming King no one would have expected or picked to win the victory. But through His death and resurrection, He is great and mighty to save.

Longing for the King

3 God's King: A Man After God's Own Heart

But what does it mean to go after God's own heart? In Psalm 18, we see a glimpse into the heart of David:

> ¹ I love You, LORD, my strength.
> ² The LORD is my rock, my fortress, and my deliverer,
> my God, my mountain where I seek refuge,
> my shield and the horn of my salvation, my stronghold.
> ³ I called to the LORD, who is worthy of praise,
> and I was saved from my enemies.
> **PSALM 18:1-3**

From this psalm we also see David's trust in God to be his strength, his rock, his fortress, his deliverer, his refuge, his shield, his salvation, and stronghold. Why would you need such things? You need strength when you're weak. You need a deliverer when you're trapped. You need a shield when you feel attacked all around. You need salvation when you're in sin. You need all of these things.

What are some actions you would expect from someone "after God's own heart"?

We see from this list that being "after God's own heart" corresponds to our humility. It comes from a place where we recognize our desperate need for God. To have a heart after God doesn't mean you are sinless. If this were the case, we would all be disqualified immediately. A heart after God doesn't mean a sinless heart; it means a repentant heart.

The difference between Saul and David wasn't that Saul was a sinner and David was sinless. David's sin was great, but his repentance outshone his sins. David's desire to return to God was greater than his desire to run away. This is how we ought to see David as an example for us. As we see David commit adultery and murder, we ought to realize that it's going to be very difficult to out-sin David.

A Future Reality

For those of you who feel like your past sins disqualify you from being a person after God's own heart, David's story gives hope. However great your sins may be, God is the faithful Deliverer who saves anyone who will trust in Him.

> Take inventory of your own heart. What are some signs of repentance in your life?

> Describe how repentance propels you forward with God.

> In what ways can you give hope to someone who has a hard time believing in God's forgiveness?

GROUP STUDY

Warm Up

Often we interpret the story of David and Goliath by putting ourselves in David's shoes, as if we are the heroes facing down the giants in our lives. If we have courage like David, we can overcome any obstacle or challenge no matter how big, and God will protect us from bad things that could happen to us. While it's true that we can and should learn from David's example of courage in this passage, such kingdom living is impossible unless it's grounded in the bigger picture—that the young king anointed by God is accomplishing a decisive victory for his people.

David isn't merely an example of what we can accomplish through our faith. He's the person God used to defeat the enemies of His people. David won the victory through God's power, not his own. This story, along with the rest of the Bible, is about how God chooses to accomplish His purposes through ordinary, sinful people like us.

When you read the stories in Scripture, how does God speak to you?

Have you ever thought, *If I had the faith of David, or the obedience of Noah, or the resolve of Joseph, then God would use me like He used them?* What's the danger in approaching the Bible like this?

What should be the "take away" when studying biblical characters?

Discussion

During this time you will have an opportunity to discuss what God revealed to you during the week. Listed below are some of the questions from your daily reading assignments. They will guide your small-group discussion.

1. What your favorite "underdog" story? Why do you like it so much?

2. In what ways are we enamored by the physical appearance of our leaders (political, spiritual, etc.)?

3. How can you judge a person's heart (in a good way)? How do you get to know someone beyond the surface of physical appearance?

4. In what ways does God's Word free us from judging ourselves based on appearances?

5. How does the Enemy try to intimidate you into giving up before the battle begins?

6. Take inventory of your own heart. What are some signs of repentance in your life?

7. Describe how repentance propels you forward with God.

Conclusion

Through the life of David, we see God's chosen king who honors God and fights for his people. When we step back and look at the big picture of the Bible, we see how God later sent the ultimate King. We would've overlooked this King with our own eyes. His physical appearance wasn't overpowering, but He walked in power. He knew His Father, and He offers redemption and victory. In every sense of the expression, King Jesus was a man "after God's own heart." And God's heart was, is, and will always be to seek out and save those who are lost.

Like David, all earthly kings are imperfect representations of the perfect King of kings. The Old Testament looked forward to the coming of this King, His people today look back to His coming, and they also look forward to His second coming. We are always longing for this King.

Spend some time praying this for you and for your group:

> "God, may You teach me how to be a person after Your heart. Remind me when I judge others because of their appearance. Give me the grace to repent and return to You. I want to walk with You, and become more like Christ."

---

1. D. A. Carson, *For the Love of God*, vol. 1 (Wheaton: Crossway, 2006), 25.
2. Dirk Philips, *Concerning Spiritual Restitution*, in *Early Anabaptist Spirituality: Selected Writings*, trans. and ed. Daniel Liechty, 236.

> Our spiritual David, Jesus Christ, in his divine righteousness has taken away our sin and slew death with his eternal life ... That is the joyous gospel with which the Holy Spirit comforts all repentant and troubled hearts.[2]
>
> **DIRK PHILIPS (1504–1568)**

NOTES

SMALL-GROUP TIPS

Reading through this section and utilizing the suggested principles and practices will greatly enhance the group experience. First is to accept your limitations. You cannot transform a life. Your group must be devoted to the Bible, the Holy Spirit, and the power of Christian community. In doing so your group will have all the tools necessary to draw closer to God and to each other—and to experience heart transformation.

GENERAL TIPS:

- Prepare for each meeting by reviewing the material, praying for each group member, and asking the Holy Spirit to work through you as you point to Jesus each week.

- Make new attendees feel welcome.

- Think of ways to connect with group members away from group time. The amount of participation you have during your group meetings is directly related to the amount of time you connect with your group members away from the group meeting. Consider sending e-mails, texts, or social networking messages encouraging members in their personal devotion times prior to the session.

MATERIALS NEEDED:

- Bible

- Bible study book

- Pen/pencil

PROVIDE RESOURCES FOR GUESTS:

- An inexpensive way to make first-time guests feel welcome is to provide them a copy of your Bible study book. Estimate how many first-time guests you can expect during the course of your study, and secure that number of books. What about people who have not yet visited your group? You can encourage them to visit by providing a copy of the Bible study book.

SMALL-GROUP VALUES

Meeting together to study God's Word and experience life together is an exciting adventure. Here are values to consider for small-group experiences:

COMMUNITY: God is relational, so He created us to live in relationship with Him and one another. Authentic community involves sharing life together and connecting on many levels with others in our group.

INTERACTIVE BIBLE STUDY: God gave the Bible as our instruction manual for life. We need to deepen our understanding of God's Word. People learn and remember more as they wrestle with truth and learn from others. Bible discovery and group interaction will enhance spiritual growth.

EXPERIENTIAL GROWTH: Beyond solely reading, studying, and dissecting the Bible, being a disciple of Christ involves marrying knowledge and experience. We do this by taking questions to God, opening a dialogue with our hearts, and utilizing other ways to listen to God speak (other people, nature, circumstances, etc.). Experiential growth is always grounded in the Bible as God's primary revelation and our ultimate truth-source.

POWER OF GOD: Processes and strategies will be ineffective unless we invite and embrace the presence and power of God. In order to experience community and growth, Jesus needs to be the centerpiece of our group experiences, and the Holy Spirit must be at work.

REDEMPTIVE COMMUNITY: Healing best occurs within the context of community and relationships. It's vital to see ourselves through the eyes of others, share our stories, and ultimately find freedom from the secrets and lies that enslave our souls.

MISSION: God has invited us into a larger story with a great mission of setting captives free and healing the broken-hearted (see Isa. 61:1-2). However, we can only join in this mission to the degree that we've let Jesus bind up our wounds and set us free. Others will be attracted to an authentic, redemptive community.

Continue the journey with The Gospel Project® ongoing studies...

Enjoying The Gospel Project?
If your group meets regularly, consider adopting
The Gospel Project as an ongoing Bible study series.

NEW STUDIES RELEASE EVERY THREE MONTHS.

Web: gospelproject.com
Twitter: @Gospel_Project
Facebook: TheGospelProject